Copyright

Bravery Unleashed: Redefining Courage and Igniting Personal Growth

© 2025 by Lesley D. Nurse

All rights reserved. No part of this publication may be reproduced, distributed, or transmitted in any form or by any means, including photocopying, recording, or other electronic or mechanical methods, without prior written permission of the publisher, except for brief quotations used in reviews or critical articles.

Published by 7Seven Spark Publishing

www.LesleyNurse.com | www.7SevenSparkPublishing.com

ISBN 979-8-218-23540-6

Printed in the United States of America

First Edition

Unlock Your Destiny

Dear Friend,

I am thrilled to present this workbook to you, a testament to your worthiness of a life filled with boundless possibilities. Within these pages lies the key to unlocking the life you desire in every aspect. Whatever you may have felt lacking or uncertain about, know that it is now within your grasp. The time has come for you to rise above your doubts and fears and step into your power.

Consider this support as a precious gift, waiting patiently inside you to be claimed. It's a reminder that you possess the strength, the courage, and the resilience to conquer any challenge that comes your way. As you embark on this journey of self-discovery, let this be your companion, guiding you toward a future, joy, and fulfillment.

Believe in yourself, dear friend, for you are capable of achieving greatness. Take this to tap into the limitless potential within you and watch as your dreams unfold before your very eyes. The time is now. The new _you_ that you desire awaits. Embrace your destiny, and let it be a testament to the incredible person you are.

With warm regards,

Lesley

WHEN YOU THINK OF
BEING BRAVE,
WHAT COMES TO MIND?

_____
_____
_____
_____
_____
_____
_____
_____

Is it being bold and daring? Or speaking your mind and standing up for others or yourself?

_____
_____
_____
_____
_____

WHERE DID I GET
MY DEFINITION OF BEING BRAVE?

During my own evolution and spending time in social solitude, I had the chance to learn what has shifted for me and my view on bravery.

Defining Bravery: A Personal Journey

Where did I get my definition of being brave?

Growing up and feeling defenseless in toxic, abusive relationships, I didn't realize the redefinition of what bravery would mean to me at the end of that era.

I SET IN STONE THE FIRMNESS, SETTING BOUNDARIES, AND NOT LETTING ANYONE WHO SHOWED A SHRED OF AGGRESSION OR MANIPULATION GET THE BEST OF ME.

Adversity into Empower

I remember when

Adversity into Empower

Adversity into Empower

Adversity into Empower

Adversity into Empower

Looking back now

Adversity into Empower

Adversity into Empower

Adversity into Empower

Breaking the Cycle: Elevating Bravery

I thought this was the one cure-all for everything.

Instead

Adversity into Empower

Adversity into Empower

Adversity into Empower

Adversity into Empower

But this proved to be too much whenever I faced a challenge from men who resembled patterns of my past. Even though I didn't raise my voice most times,

if they trembled my way- they were in for trouble. There was this survival rule that I made up and stuck to - until I realized I didn't want to deal with this path anymore. Instead, I tried to claim my untapped peace.

MY UNTAPPED PEACE

4-Week Focus Outcome

_____

_____

Main Tasks Week 1

1. _____

_____

2. _____

_____

3. _____

_____

Notes:

_____

_____

_____

_____

Today's Tasks

1. _____

_____

2. _____

_____

3. _____

_____

Dump Zone
Projects & Ideas for later

_____

_____

_____

_____

_____

_____

_____

_____

_____

_____

_____

Weekly Goal: _____

INTENTION VS WHAT I DO

At times, we intend to do or say something but end up doing or saying something else entirely. This exercise aims to break habitual patterns and assist in aligning one's words with their intended meaning.

I MEANT	VS	(I DO) ACTIONS

INTENTION VS WHAT I DO

At times, we intend to do or say something but end up doing or saying something else entirely. This exercise aims to break habitual patterns and assist in aligning one's words with their intended meaning.

I MEANT	VS	(I DO) ACTIONS

I LEARNED THAT ONE ENGAGEMENT OF NEGATIVITY COULD SPIRAL OUT OF CONTROL AND GROW INTO SOMETHING THAT CAN FESTER - BEYOND YOUR MOMENTARY FRUSTRATIONS.

You could be the type that gets over it, but the other person might not, and then it's rounds 2, 3, and 4 until forever. So how do you break the cycle? You elevate being brave.

Adversity into Empower

I remember when

Adversity into Empower

Adversity into Empower

Adversity into Empower

Adversity into Empower

Looking back now

Adversity into Empower

Adversity into Empower

Adversity into Empower

Breaking the Cycle: Elevating Bravery

I thought this was the one cure-all for everything.

Instead
_____
_____
_____
_____
_____
_____
_____

Adversity into Empower

Adversity into Empower

Adversity into Empower

Unlock Your Destiny

When I would stand up for myself, it would rarely be cut and dry. The other person would have their say, other people would get involved, and it would turn into a mess in some form that wasted time.

Unlock Your Destiny

It's not to say this happens quite often, but if something needed to be addressed, that was it. Things changed when I realized I was losing untapped happiness.

Unlock Your Destiny

When I get upset or speak on behalf of my trauma to someone else, only someone who has survived the same past traumas can understand how difficult that can be.

MY UNTAPPED PEACE

4-Week Focus Outcome

_____
_____

Main Tasks Week 2

1. _____
   _____
2. _____
   _____
3. _____
   _____

Notes:

_____
_____
_____
_____

Today's Tasks

1. _____
   _____
2. _____
   _____
3. _____
   _____

Dump Zone
Projects & Ideas for later

_____
_____
_____
_____
_____
_____
_____
_____
_____
_____

Weekly Goal: _____

Unlock Your Destiny

You don't see an argument or someone taking advantage of you in the same way as someone who has not had shared experiences. Fighting the trauma that you see through their aggression then becomes your bullseye.

ADVERSITY INTO EMPOWER

I remember when

Adversity into Empower

Adversity into Empower

Adversity into Empower

Adversity into Empower

Looking back now

Adversity into Empower

Adversity into Empower

Adversity into Empower

Breaking the Cycle: Elevating Bravery

I thought this was the one cure-all for everything.

Instead _____
_____
_____
_____
_____
_____
_____
_____

color

Adversity into Empower

Adversity into Empower

Adversity into Empower

Adversity into Empower

MY UNTAPPED PEACE

4-Week Focus Outcome

Today's Tasks

1. ----------------------------

----

2. ----------------------------

----

3. ----------------------------

Main Tasks Week 3

1. ----------------------------

----

2. ----------------------------

----

3. ----------------------------

Notes:

Dump Zone
Projects & Ideas for later

Weekly Goal: --------------------------------

Unlock Your Destiny

WHAT BRAVERY TRULY
ENTAILS

I wanted more joy.

Unlock Your Destiny

IT'S ONE THING TO KNOW BETTER, BUT IT'S ANOTHER THING WHEN YOU ARE A WORK IN PROGRESS TRYING TO MATCH YOUR ACTIONS WITH YOUR MIND.

Adversity into Empower

Unlock Your Destiny

Just because you missed the ball doesn't mean you haven't tried; it takes time to break habits and patterns, which I possessed and struggled to let go of.

ADVERSITY into Empower

I remember when

Adversity into Empower

Adversity into Empower

Adversity into Empower

Adversity into Empower

Looking back now

Adversity into Empower

Adversity into Empower

Adversity into Empower

Breaking the Cycle: Elevating Bravery

I thought this was the one cure-all for everything.

Instead

Adversity into Empower

Adversity into Empower

Adversity into Empower

Adversity into Empower

MY UNTAPPED PEACE

4-Week Focus Outcome

_____
_____

Main Tasks Week 4

1. _____
_____

2. _____
_____

3. _____
_____

Notes:

_____
_____
_____
_____

Today's Tasks

1. _____
_____

2. _____
_____

3. _____

Dump Zone
Projects & Ideas for later

_____
_____
_____
_____
_____
_____
_____
_____
_____
_____
_____
_____

Weekly Goal: _____

Unlock Your Destiny

UNWAVERING KINDNESS: A PILLAR OF BRAVERY

What I learned about being brave once I had a better handle on it.

Adversity into Empower

Unlock Your Destiny

Being brave is not about being necessarily bold in the tone of your voice but in the steps that you take in life and the ones you refuse.

ADVERSITY INTO EMPOWER

Unlock Your Destiny

INSTEAD, YOU GIVE YOURSELF TIME TO LISTEN FIRST AND ACT LATER. IT'S ABOUT ALLOWING MATURITY TO MATERIALIZE INSTEAD OF GIVING IN TO YOUR IMMEDIATE DESIRES AND HABITS.

Adversity into Empower

Unlock Your Destiny

It's about the boundaries you set and commit to, which no one can cross. It's about reserving your tongue and thoughts and not being quick to react or get lost in overthinking

Adversity into Empower

Unlock Your Destiny

BEING BRAVE IS ABOUT BEING KIND AND LOVING TO YOURSELF AND OTHERS DESPITE BEING PASSED OVER, WRONGED, OR THINGS THAT DIDN'T GO YOUR WAY;

Adversity into Empower

Unlock Your Destiny

It's about taking the wins and losses, seeing them as lessons, and pushing forward. To be brave is, to be honest, aware, soft-spoken, and unwavering in your spirit. It does not feed your ego – it fuels your soul.

ADVERSITY INTO EMPOWER

I remember when

Adversity into Empower

Adversity into Empower

Adversity into Empower

Adversity into Empower

Adversity into Empower

Looking back now

Adversity into Empower

Adversity into Empower

Adversity into Empower

Breaking the Cycle: Elevating Bravery

I thought this was the one cure-all for everything.

Instead _____
_____
_____
_____
_____
_____
_____

Adversity into Empower

Adversity into Empower

Adversity into Empower

Adversity into Empower

Adversity into Empower

color

Unlock Your Destiny

The Multitude of Bravery

Unlock Your Destiny

To be brave is to take steps forward despite feeling uncertain inside. It's not about transferring your emotional bags onto others, lashing out and deflecting, or simply using buzzwords to take ownership of missteps.

Unlock Your Destiny

It's about learning, relearning, and committing to doing better. Being brave is about being loving to yourself even if you are not happy with your progress in life – you root for yourself anyway. Being brave is about being steady, kind, and open-minded, despite what is happening.

Unlock Your Destiny

EMBRACE PERSONAL
GROWTH WITH GRACE

Unlock Your Destiny

While it might sound ideal to some, it is doable and doesn't mean that you are not brave if you don't do everything listed or in order. Give yourself grace, time, and room to grow, is the bravest gift of all.

Unlock Your Destiny

IF YOU ARE STRUGGLING TO BREAK OUT OF OUTDATED PATTERNS AND THOUGHTS, KNOW THAT IT IS POSSIBLE.

Unlock Your Destiny

CONCLUSION

Bravery is an act of commitment

Conclusion, bravery and commitment are intertwined in a beautiful dance of self-discovery and purpose. Bravery is not just a momentary act, but a continuous commitment to embracing challenges, pushing boundaries, and striving for personal enlightenment.

When we commit ourselves to becoming the best version of ourselves, even the most ordinary tasks become extraordinary. It is through this unwavering dedication that we find true fulfillment and meaning in our lives. So, let us embrace bravery and commitment, for they hold the key to unlocking our potential and living a life of purpose.

COURSE WORKBOOK

MINDSET QUIZ

There's no right or wrong answer here — just awareness. Every choice reveals something about how you face challenge and change.

WHAT IS AN ACT OF BEING BRAVE?

- INSTIGATING
- RAGE
- TRYING AGAIN
- GOSSIPPING

WHAT IS AN EXAMPLE OF **NOT** ENGAGING?

- ARGUING
- IGNORING
- GASLIGHTING
- COVERT RETALIATION ACTS

SELECT ACTS OF BRAVERY

- KINDNESS
- LETTING GO
- TANTRUMS
- RESERVED
- SPEAKING UP
- NOT ENGAGING
- AUTHENTIC
- SELF LOVE
- MIRRORING
- REVENGE
- TRANSFERENCE
- ENVY

LESLEY D. NURSE

WWW.LESLEYNURSE.COM

BREAK FREE AND CREATE YOUR DREAM LIFE

Lesley D. Nurse is a dynamic force dedicated to empowering individuals to break free from limitation and unlock their true potential.

With a burning passion for helping others, Lesley has made it her mission to help people create the life they desire.

Through her inspiring books and creative pursuits, she invites readers on a transformative journey of self-discovery and personal growth.

Her words resonate with authenticity, wisdom, and a deep understanding of the human experience.

www.LesleyNurse.com | www.7SevenSparkPublishing.com

Break Free and Create Your Dream Life

Lesley is a dynamic force dedicated to empowering individuals to break free from the shackles of their own limitations and unlock their true potential. With a burning passion for helping others, Lesley has made it her life's mission for people to create the life they desire.

With her captivating books and numerous other pursuits, Lesley invites you to embark on a transformative journey of self-discovery and personal growth. Her words resonate with authenticity, wisdom, and a deep understanding of the human experience.

info@7sevensparkpublishing.com   www.7sevensparkpublishing.com

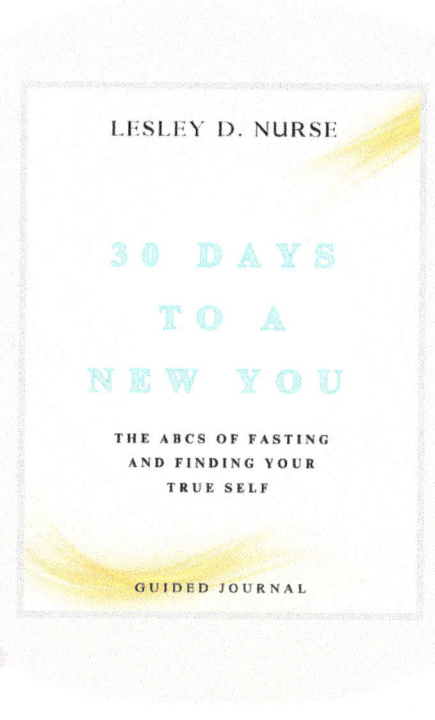

Fasting and Finding Your True Self

30 Days to a New You: The ABCs of Fasting and Finding Your True Self

This guided prompt journal helps you pause, reflect, and fast from negativity to rediscover clarity and purpose.

Each daily entry offers simple reflection steps to strengthen gratitude and self-discipline — transforming your mindset in just 30 days.

Available wherever books are sold.

www.7sevensparkpublishing.com

UNLOCK YOUR DESTINY

Daily Journal

DATES :   MOOD :

....

....

....

....

....

....

....

GOAL   TO DO LIST

UNLOCK YOUR DESTINY

Daily Journal

DATES : MOON :

....

....

....

....

....

....

....

....

....

....

UNLOCK YOUR DESTINY

Daily Journal

DATES : MOON :

....

....

....

....

....

....

....

....

....

....

....

....

UNLOCK YOUR DESTINY

Daily Journal

DATES :   **MOOD :**

....

....

....

....

....

....

....

....

....

....

....

....

UNLOCK YOUR DESTINY

Daily Journal

DATES :   MOOD :

....

....

....

....

....

....

GOAL   TO DO LIST

UNLOCK YOUR DESTINY

Daily Journal

DATES :   **MOOD :**

....

....

....

....

....

....

....

....

....

....

....

....

....

UNLOCK YOUR DESTINY

Daily Journal

DATES :   **MOOD :**

....

....

....

....

....

....

....

....

....

....

....

....

....

UNLOCK YOUR DESTINY

Daily Journal

DATES :   MOOD :

....

....

....

....

....

....

....

....

....

....

....

....

UNLOCK YOUR DESTINY

Daily Journal

DATES :   MOOD :

....

....

....

....

....

....

....

....

....

....

....

....

UNLOCK YOUR DESTINY
Daily Journal

DATES :   **MOOD :**

....

....

....

....

....

....

....

....

....

....

....

....

UNLOCK YOUR DESTINY

Daily Journal

DATES :   MOOD :

....

....

....

....

....

....

....

GOAL   TO DO LIST

UNLOCK YOUR DESTINY

Daily Journal

DATES : **MOOD :**

....

....

....

....

....

....

....

....

....

....

....

UNLOCK YOUR DESTINY
Daily Journal

DATES :   MOOD :

....

....

....

....

....

....

....

....

....

....

....

....

UNLOCK YOUR DESTINY

Daily Journal

DATES :   **MOOD :**

UNLOCK YOUR DESTINY

Daily Journal

DATES :   MOOD :

....

....

....

....

....

....

....

....

....

....

....

UNLOCK YOUR DESTINY
Daily Journal

DATES :   **MOOD :**

....

....

....

....

....

....

....

....

....

....

....

UNLOCK YOUR DESTINY

Daily Journal

DATES : MOOD :

....

....

....

....

....

....

....

GOAL TO DO LIST

UNLOCK YOUR DESTINY

Daily Journal

DATES :   MOOD :

UNLOCK YOUR DESTINY

Daily Journal

DATES :   MOOD :

UNLOCK YOUR DESTINY

Daily Journal

DATES : MOOD :

....
....
....
....
....
....
....
....
....
....
....
....

UNLOCK YOUR DESTINY

Daily Journal

DATES :   MOOD :

....

....

....

....

....

....

....

....

....

....

....

....

....

UNLOCK YOUR DESTINY

Daily Journal

DATES :   MOOD :

....

....

....

....

....

....

....

....

....

....

....

UNLOCK YOUR DESTINY
Daily Journal

DATES :   MOOD :

....

....

....

....

....

....

....

GOAL   TO DO LIST

UNLOCK YOUR DESTINY

Daily Journal

DATES :   MOOD :

....

....

....

....

....

....

....

....

....

....

UNLOCK YOUR DESTINY

Daily Journal

DATES : MOON :

....

....

....

....

....

....

....

....

....

....

....

....

....

UNLOCK YOUR DESTINY
Daily Journal

DATES : **MOOD :**

....

....

....

....

....

....

....

....

....

....

....

....

UNLOCK YOUR DESTINY

Daily Journal

DATES :   MOOD :

UNLOCK YOUR DESTINY
Daily Journal

DATES :   **MOOD :**

....

....

....

....

....

....

....

....

....

....

....

....

....

UNLOCK YOUR DESTINY

Daily Journal

DATES :   **MOOD :**

....

....

....

....

....

....

....

....

....

....

....

....

....

UNLOCK YOUR DESTINY
Daily Journal

DATES :   **MOOD :**

....

....

....

....

....

....

....

....

....

....

....

....

UNLOCK YOUR DESTINY

Daily Journal

DATES :   **MOOD :**

....

....

....

....

....

....

....

....

....

....

....

UNLOCK YOUR DESTINY

Daily Journal

DATES : MOOD :

UNLOCK YOUR DESTINY

Daily Journal

DATES :   MOOD :

....

....

....

....

....

....

....

....

....

....

....

....

UNLOCK YOUR DESTINY
Daily Journal

DATES :   **MOOD :**

....

....

....

....

....

....

....

....

....

....

....

UNLOCK YOUR DESTINY

Daily Journal

DATES :   MOOD :

....

....

....

....

....

....

....

....

....

....

....

....

UNLOCK YOUR DESTINY

Daily Journal

DATES :   MOOD :

....
....
....
....
....
....
....
....
....
....
....
....

UNLOCK YOUR DESTINY

Daily Journal

DATES :   **MOOD :**

....

....

....

....

....

....

....

....

....

....

....

....

UNLOCK YOUR DESTINY
Daily Journal

DATES :   **MOOD :**

....

....

....

....

....

....

....

....

....

....

....

....

UNLOCK YOUR DESTINY

Daily Journal

DATES :   **MOOD :**

....

....

....

....

....

....

....

....

....

....

....

....

....

UNLOCK YOUR DESTINY

Daily Journal

DATES :   MOOD :

UNLOCK YOUR DESTINY

Daily Journal

DATES :   **MOOD :**

....
....
....
....
....
....
....
....
....
....
....
....
....

UNLOCK YOUR DESTINY
Daily Journal

DATES :　　　　　　　　　　　　**MOOD :**

....

....

....

....

....

....

....

....

....

....

....

....

UNLOCK YOUR DESTINY
Daily Journal

DATES : **MOOD :**

....

....

....

....

....

....

....

....

....

....

....

UNLOCK YOUR DESTINY
Daily Journal

DATES :   MOOD :

UNLOCK YOUR DESTINY

Daily Journal

DATES :   MOOD :

....

....

....

....

....

....

....

....

....

....

....

....

UNLOCK YOUR DESTINY
Daily Journal

DATES :   **MOOD :**

....

....

....

....

....

....

....

....

....

....

....

....

UNLOCK YOUR DESTINY

Daily Journal

DATES :   MOOD :

UNLOCK YOUR DESTINY
Daily Journal

DATES :   **MOOD :**

....

....

....

....

....

....

....

....

....

....

....

....

UNLOCK YOUR DESTINY
Daily Journal

DATES :   **MOOD :**

....

....

....

....

....

....

....

....

....

....

....

....

UNLOCK YOUR DESTINY

Daily Journal

DATES :   **MOOD :**

....

....

....

....

....

....

....

....

....

....

....

....

UNLOCK YOUR DESTINY

Daily Journal

DATES :   MOOD :

....

....

....

....

....

....

....

....

....

....

....

....

....

UNLOCK YOUR DESTINY
Daily Journal

DATES : **MOOD :**

....

....

....

....

....

....

....

....

....

....

....

....

UNLOCK YOUR DESTINY

Daily Journal

DATES :   MOOD :

....

....

....

....

....

....

....

....

....

....

....

....

UNLOCK YOUR DESTINY
Daily Journal

DATES :   **MOOD :**

....

....

....

....

....

....

....

....

....

....

....

....

UNLOCK YOUR DESTINY

Daily Journal

DATES :   MOOD :

UNLOCK YOUR DESTINY
Daily Journal

DATES :   **MOOD :**

....

....

....

....

....

....

....

....

....

....

....

....

UNLOCK YOUR DESTINY

Daily Journal

DATES :   MOOD :

....

....

....

....

....

....

....

....

....

....

....

UNLOCK YOUR DESTINY
Daily Journal

DATES : **MOOD :**

....

....

....

....

....

....

....

....

....

....

....

....

UNLOCK YOUR DESTINY

Daily Journal

DATES :   **MOOD :**

....

....

....

....

....

....

....

....

....

....

....

....

UNLOCK YOUR DESTINY

Daily Journal

DATES :   MOOD :

UNLOCK YOUR DESTINY
Daily Journal

DATES :   **MOOD :**

....

....

....

....

....

....

....

....

....

....

....

....

....

www.ingramcontent.com/pod-product-compliance
Lightning Source LLC
Chambersburg PA
CBHW080549030426
42337CB00024B/4818